Go Ask Dad

Fathers are Nice Guys

Go Ask Dad

Fathers are Nice Guys

Ian Darling

Illustrated by Mike Inkol

mosaic press

National Library of Canada
Cataloguing in Publication Data

Darling, Ian, 1948-
        Go ask Dad: fathers are nice guys / Ian
        Darling; illustrated by Mike Inkol

ISBN 0-88962-835-1

1. Fathers—Humor. 2. Fatherhood—Humor. I. Title.

PN6231.F37D37 2004   C818'.602 C2004-902416-7

Published by Mosaic Press, offices and warehouse at 1252 Speers
Road, Units 1 and 2, Oakville, Ontario, L6L 5N9, Canada and Mosaic
Press, PMB 145, 4500 Witmer Industrial Estates, Niagara Falls, NY,
14305-1386, U.S.A.

Mosaic Press acknowledges the assistance of the Canada Council
and the Department of Canadian Heritage, Government of Canada
for their support of our publishing programme.

Le Conseil des Arts | The Canada Council
du Canada | for the Arts

Mosaic Press in Canada:
1252 Speers Road, Units 1 & 2,
Oakville, Ontario
L6L 5N9
Phone/Fax: 905-825-2130
info@mosaic-press.com

Mosaic Press U.S.A.:
4500 Witmer Industrial Estates
PMB 145, Niagara Falls, NY
14305-1386
Phone/Fax: 1-800-387-8992
info@mosaic-press.com

www.mosaic-press.com

For Dad

Acknowledgements

An honorable writer always acknowledges the people who helped with a book but quickly adds that they are not responsible for any errors or omissions. This sentiment is very noble but is contrary to the advice of my lawyer.

Therefore, I would like readers of this book to hold the following people responsible for anything they don't think is quite right: Sheila Hannon, a friend of mine who read the manuscript and thought it — like men — needed improvement, and Kathryn Exner, an editor who offered advice and had several opportunities to tell me not to foist the manuscript on the public.

My wife, Jane Ann, is also responsible because she encouraged me from the start. She believed I was writing a work of fiction, but all fathers will know I made absolutely nothing up.

Finally, I must mention my children, Amanda, Tamara and Caroline. If they hadn't misbehaved, I would have had far less to write about.

Ian Darling

Table of Contents

Forewarning

When I started this book, my intent was to write a few humorous lines about dads feeling less appreciated than anyone other than the taxman. If we're living in a patriarchal society, nobody bothered to tell the fathers of the world — and surely they should be informed, even if they're the last to know. Instead of fathers being in command of their families, they spend their time carrying out orders given by their kids. These are the kids who, sooner or later, are supposed to help their dads. Alas, it's always going to be later.

When I had almost finished this book, I started to wonder if this theme might upset some fathers. I feared they might not be amused when they realize that kids have no intention of giving up their power and privileges. I wondered if being lighthearted about the plight of fathers might be going too far.

Humor is not always appropriate because people take it so seriously. Nevertheless, I set aside my reservations and continued to write because I thought fathers have at least earned the right to decide when they should laugh. I know this isn't much but at least it's something.

Regardless of whether these pages are deemed to be humorous or grim, I claim only that they show Dad as he really is: devoted and hardworking, whether he wants to be or not. He gets up in the middle of the night to look after his young children when they know he should be sleeping; he listens to them sing in school concerts despite the damage it does to his eardrums, and he coaches teams of little leaguers that could never lose if they only followed his brilliant strategies.

Never once does Dad ask for a government grant, a medal or a pat on the back. The thought never occurs to him. His only compensation is watching a ballgame with his kids once or twice a year.

This, of course, isn't enough. Fathers deserve something they haven't been able to get: respect. I hope the publication of this book helps them to get it. The meritorious service performed by fathers at least seven days a week should be acknowledged not just in the men's locker room where it has always been honored, but in another sweaty institution: the United Nations, which should declare every day to be Father's Day.

Because the UN won't make this declaration if the credibility of this book is in doubt, I feel obligated to reveal my sources. I got most of my information by listening to my three children: Amanda, Tamara and Caroline. Because I expect them to deny everything, I checked my observations with other fathers. It was unanimous. They all agreed with me. It's amazing how dads think alike. You'd think they all go through the same trials and tribulations. I should acknowledge that I did not seek the counsel of anyone other than fathers. This wasn't because I was not interested in presenting two sides of this story but because I feared anything that anyone other than fathers said on this subject would be biased.

Now that this book is finished, I shall be devoting my full attention again to my regular job as an editorial writer in Kitchener, where I write about other amusing subjects such as the way our politicians are solving world problems. But I have had no reprieve from my other job: helping to look after my three kids. Despite the urgent need to complete this manuscript, they expected me to chauffeur them around town, feed them on a regular basis and do their homework. As always, I did what I was told.

Ian Darling,
Waterloo, Ont.

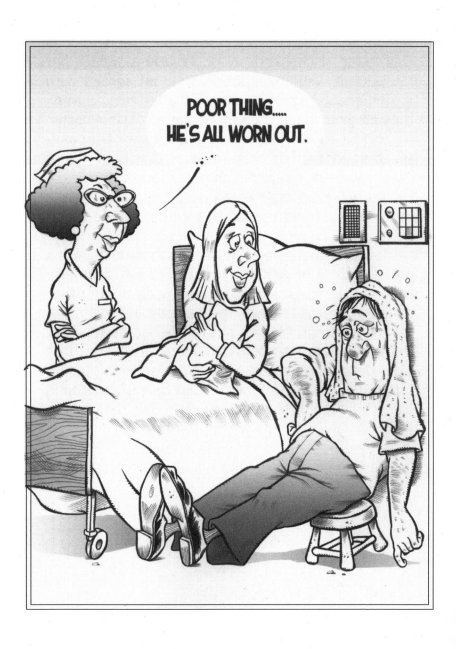

Delivery Boys

The role of fathers in the birth of children has been unappreciated. Women think they are the most important people in the birthing process and men have been too modest to correct this misperception.

The truth is that men start getting ready to deliver babies long before women even begin to think about it. As teenagers, boys intuitively understand that the day will come when everything will depend upon their ability to drive to a hospital as quickly as Jeff Gordon drives at a racetrack. This explains why teenage boys rev their cars and squeal their tires. Their conduct has usually been regarded as immature and treated with contempt: "They're just showing off to their girlfriends." Nonsense. How else are they supposed to demonstrate their driving skills to girls who will require them one day? How else is the human race supposed to survive?

When the big day comes, Dad is ready. It doesn't matter if it's in the middle of the night and he would rather sleep. It doesn't matter if it's cold outside and he would rather stay indoors. It doesn't even matter if the roads are bad. Dad rises to the challenge and gets Mom to the closest hospital. Even after arriving at hospital, Dad cannot rest. Far from it. His duties are vital. While Mom is huffing and puffing, he has to tell the clerk in the admitting room that his wife is there to have a baby. Think about it. The doctors couldn't help a woman to deliver her baby if someone didn't explain what she needed. What are the doctors supposed to do — guess what the problem is?

Most fathers perform their role in the admitting department very well. The only time they are not sure what to say occurs when the clerk runs through all the questions on the form and asks if the patient is there as a result of an accident.

The chores of driving to the hospital and filling out the forms used to be perceived as so strenuous that, after they were done, men were encouraged to relax in the hospital corridors while their wives moved into the delivery room. Since the '70s, fathers have been expected to help in the delivery room too. Oh well, what's one more job? Besides, they have been well prepared for this part of the procedure by attending pre-natal classes. They paid close attention when the instructor showed them how to help their wives breathe deeply. They have to suck in and then blow out. Apparently, women forget to breathe while they are in labor.

After it's all over, Dad still has to perform the time-consuming task of phoning his wife's mother, sisters, aunts and every girlfriend she has had since kindergarten. This is all quite exhausting. As he recounts the events of the day, he never acknowledges the role he played. As always, he's too modest.

Dad Can Rock Babies

Even though Dad knows he has the ability to help take care of babies because he was once one himself, no one else seems to have much faith in him — not even Mom.

When Dad's little boy or girl is crying in the night or needs a bath, he knows what to do: delegate. Assigning tasks to others is a sign of good management. This is particularly true if the baby needs a clean diaper.

Surprisingly, Mom does not appreciate this management style and points out that good managers are prepared to do the tasks they ask others to do. Dad, always being fair, acknowledges that that concept has some validity, some of the time.

The only task she trusts him to do on his own is to find the baby's pacifier. She has noticed that the mere threat of the baby crying sends Dad racing through the house on a pacifier hunt.

As the days and weeks go by and he demonstrates that he can look after the baby as well as he can delegate, he still feels slighted. Now, for example, when he is trying to rock the baby to sleep, he is accused of handling the baby like a football. Dad doesn't understand the problem. He never fumbled the ball in high school.

No matter how many times he has fed the baby with a bottle, he is still told to warm it first and to burp the baby later. And no matter how many times Mom leaves the baby with him when she goes out, she repeats the same long description of how he should put the baby to bed. This is not necessary. Although he might not get as much sleep as he did before the baby was born, there is nothing wrong with his memory.

Dad stoically concludes that if he were a pediatrician in charge of the children's ward at a major hospital, at home he would be told his medical education was second rate because he never learned the words to a lullaby he's supposed to sing as he rocks the baby.

When Mom gets a cold, however, Dad takes over and does a wonderful job looking after the baby, who not only survives but appears to enjoy the rock songs Dad sings instead of lullabies. Mom now has some faith in him, some of the time.

The Joke Is On The Kids

Dad's sense of humor is usually misunderstood. This is no laughing matter.

His jokes never produce anything but groans. "Why are astronauts always being arrested? — Because they keep defying the law of gravity." Groan. "How do prison inmates plan their escapes? — With cell phones." Groan, groan. "Why does a fisherman always know how heavy a fish is? — Fish come with scales." Groan, groan, groan.

The only people who appreciate his humor are other fathers. They understand. Women think something isn't funny unless it makes men look silly. You know the kind of lines they like: "The perfect woman, the perfect man, the Easter bunny and Santa Claus were in a car when a tire blew. Who got out to fix it? The perfect woman — because the other three are just a figment of your imagination."

Ha. ha. Granted, jokes such as this make the writers for late-night talk shows rich, but they are forgotten five minutes after they are uttered. The talk-show writers should stand in awe of every father who can get up and deliver lines that will be remembered all evening for bringing the house down, albeit with groans. In response, Dad naturally says that if the house has come down, he will be staying home from work so he can put it back up. Groan, groan, groan, groan.

Dad's harmless corny jokes serve the vital purpose of promoting peace among warring factions in the family. By creating a cheerful mood without upsetting anybody, they reduce the tension that would otherwise arise during debates on difficult subjects such as who gets to see which show on television. Because of this accomplishment, Dad does not deserve the rolled eyes his jokes prompt. He deserves the Nobel Peace Prize. Nothing could be a more serious matter.

Toying With Construction

When Dad brings home a box containing a swing set, he hopes that the kids will be occupied for hours, thereby keeping them out of trouble and discouraging them from watching the mindless television shows of no redeeming value that they like to watch. Instead, he finds the task of building the backyard playground so daunting that he becomes occupied for hours, thereby keeping him out of trouble and discouraging *him* from watching the mindless television shows of no redeeming value that he likes to watch.

Even though the swing set comes with instructions, Dad doesn't bother to look at them because he is sure he has enough experience from his junior high shop class. After several frustrating hours of trying to fit parts together that were never meant to be connected, he decides that reading the instructions may, in fact, be helpful.

He quickly notes, however, that they are written in about 75 different languages. Of course, there is nothing wrong with this. The problem is finding something in the language used at home. When one of the kids points out the section in English, Dad says that he doesn't call that English but gobbledygook written by some guys who studied engineering but who either failed English 101 or never took it. The instructions, he declares, make no sense, are incomplete and could never be fully deciphered by anyone who isn't an engineer. The only phrase he recognizes is "some assembly required."

He has to spend another couple of hours translating the rest of the instructions into something he can understand. Finally, Dad is ready to build, but he now has a new problem. He doesn't have the wrenches, pliers and hammers required for the job. This, too, he declares the fault of the engineers. They wrote the instructions without knowing what tools he has in his basement. To make matters worse, the instructions state that if the proper tools are not used, the warranty will be null and void, and he knows his kids are likely to sue him, not the manufacturer, over any fault, real or imagined, that arises if the swing set is not assembled properly.

In desperation, Dad decides to visit his next-door neighbor, who points out that Dad's ability to complete the swing set would greatly improve if he stays for a glass of beer, another item the instructions failed to mention. Armed now with both the appropriate lubricant and the neighbor's tools, Dad goes home to complete a project he regards as comparable to the erection in New York of the Statue of Liberty. It, too, required some assembling after it arrived. As he tightens the last nuts and bolts, he imagines the swing set standing as a neighborhood icon long after he is gone. Dad is so inspired he doesn't hear Mom calling him for dinner or notice when the streetlights come on. Finally, his work is finished. He calls the kids. Instead of the joy and wonder he anticipates, they refuse to come. They are too busy playing in the cardboard box the swing set arrived in.

Big Mac's Attack On Taste

Whenever the family is in the car and everyone starts to get hungry, Dad drives as far away as he possibly can from any McDonald's restaurant. He must be miles from any golden arches when he asks, "Where should we go to eat?" He knows the answer the kids will give, and he knows his only defence is to be able to say in all honesty that there is no McDonald's within 10 miles.

When he does go to McDonald's, Dad knows that he isn't going to see filet mignon or coq au vin on the menu, or even a wine list. He's stuck with a Big Mac, fries and a coffee. This never tempts his appetite, but he's not surprised that McDonald's can put up the sign that says it has served billions and billions of hamburgers: his kids are responsible for a significant number of those sales.

But Dad doesn't understand McDonald's. He thinks the point of going to a restaurant is to eat food.

That's nonsense. The kids know the real purpose. It is to have fun, and McDonald's knows how to provide it. Ronald McDonald may not know much about food, but he does know something about kids. Some McDonald's have playgrounds with more caves and tubes than a five-year-old can count, let alone explore, and they offer cute toys built to a standard far higher than a Big Mac.

But if Dad can't count on McDonald's to stimulate his taste buds, he can count on it to provide friendly service from smiling employees. Everyone who has anything to do with McDonald's smiles. It's no wonder these people are always smiling. They've been able to get Dad to part with his hard-earned money to buy a miserable Big Mac.

But, maybe, it's Dad who gets the last smile. He knows that when the kids bring their new McDonald's toys into the car, they will be quiet for 10 minutes. This is worth at least as much as filet mignon.

The Chauffeur

Before a wedding, the groom is supposed to pick up a marriage licence at city hall, but if he plans to be a father eventually, he should be required to get a chauffeur's licence as well. In the long run, this licence would be more beneficial.

The need for a chauffeur's licence becomes clear when the first child is about four. This is when kids start learning how to hit a baseball, play the piano or do a pirouette. Every family has a different combination of sporting activities and cultural lessons, but most have a common denominator: The teachers, leaders and coaches expect the kids to come to them rather than the other way around. This isn't fair, but by now Dad realizes that few people have his sense of fairness. This means Dad has to drive. And drive. And drive.

True, Mom has been known to do some of the driving, but on a Saturday morning when a parent must drive kids to different locations all over town, there isn't any doubt who has the skill for this thankless task. It is Dad. The same skill that was required to race through town to get to the hospital delivery room is in demand once again.

He must not fail. If he is even two minutes late for a practice, he is accused by his kids of ruining the entire event they are practising for. Even if the roads are busy because all fathers are driving their children to lessons, Dad hears from the back seat that he, personally, will be responsible for this calamity, which he is made to feel will mark a low point in the history of Western civilization. If he is late for one practice, he has a compounding problem. He will also be late for the next activity, which is miles away. This will mark an even lower point in history.

Unfortunately, police departments do not understand Dad's tight schedule or the importance of the events he is trying to get to. They regularly hand out speeding tickets to him when he is just doing his job. Police officers would be better off to leave him alone. They should know that what they are doing is cruel and unusual punishment.

Rather than stopping Dad, the police should provide a cruiser with a siren and flashing lights to lead his car as quickly as possible through the streets. His only sin is that he is doing the job of a chauffeur without the appropriate licence.

Dad Needs A Page

Whenever Dad goes into a bookstore, he realizes that he'll have a problem. At present, many books deal with unimportant matters, such as how to retire with $1 million on an initial investment of $2.99. That's nice to know, but Dad is more interested in seeking advice that will help him survive until he retires; he can worry about money in his next life.

There must be some writers around with real life experience who could jot down a few thoughts that would help Dad. One popular title would be, *Do As I Say, Not As I Do*. This book would be particularly appreciated by dads who smoke, gamble and drink. They know that what they are doing is wrong; they just don't know why that should be held against them if they tell their kids to stay on the straight and narrow path.

Another title would be, *You Can Trust People Over 30*. This theme has been on Dad's mind ever since his 30th birthday. He knows that the concept of not trusting anyone over that age sprang up in the '60s. It may have been true then, but that's no reason for his kids to throw it back at him now. The baby boomers discovered when they turned 30 that they inexplicably remained trustworthy, unlike the previous generation.

A third book would be taken by Dad whenever he drives the family to a place he hasn't previously visited, *I'm Not Lost, I Just Like To Take My Time*. No further elaboration is needed.

There is one book that Dad would particularly like to see written, *How Dad Can Get The Time He Needs To Read Everything He Wants To Read*. This book would provide a real solution to a real problem, but the bookstores may be reluctant to stock it because they may suspect that fathers won't have the time to read it.

Work Begins In The Evening

After a hard day at the office or plant, fathers have to do their real work: their kids' homework. This is a major change from the past when children were expected to finish their assignments on their own. But kids are now far too busy with extracurricular activities to have any time for homework. They therefore assume a managerial role and tell Dad what he has to do in order for them to get an A on all their assignments.

So, despite being tired and worn out, Dad has to write a review of a book he doesn't want to read, produce a replica of an 18th century fort, and finish a science project that shows some phenomenon such as why an apple falls when he personally doesn't care if Isaac Newton had never told anyone about the law of gravity.

Placing this burden upon fathers to do the grunt work should prompt a reassessment of the concept

of homework. If the teachers can't teach students how to do assignments during the school day, they should be the ones who do the extra work. They should make house calls every night to help the kids. The most that can be said for these assignments is that they act as refresher courses for Dad. Because he's forgotten everything he ever learned at school, he has no alternative but to go to the local library to ask for help doing "his" school project. Understandably, he feels a bit sheepish when he makes this request, but librarians, being sensitive individuals, happily help because they know that Dad is just doing his job and he shouldn't be teased about it.

It is probably true that most fathers take these assignments in stride and do them without complaining. It would be nice, however, during the school assembly at the end of the year if the principal would acknowledge Dad's contribution to the education system. Without his help, his kids would never have accomplished so much and the teachers would never have the satisfaction of thinking they had done a great job.

Dad, however, does have the satisfaction of knowing when the assembly is over that he may relax for a few months until he has to do his homework again in September.

The Concert Master

The Christmas concert at school is one of the best methods ever invented of educating people. Dad learns lessons at it that he will never forget.

First, he learns that he cannot offer any excuses for being late for an important event. It doesn't matter if his company has just named him chief executive officer and asked him to call the president in the White House, he's supposed to be home in time to get changed and drive to the school in a relaxed, cheerful mood. Furthermore, he cannot blame heavy traffic, road construction, hurricanes, tornadoes or earthquakes. He's supposed to anticipate problems and plan his day accordingly.

Second, Dad learns patience. He has to sit and pretend to enjoy all the Grade 1, 2 and 3 students endlessly singing songs about Suzy Snowflake or some other flake. And he has to pay sufficient attention that he remembers to clap at the right times.

The third lesson is that Dad cannot snooze during the concert no matter how many times he yawns. He is not even allowed to close his eyes. If he falls asleep and misses his kid's performance, he'll be in real trouble.

The fourth lesson is how to endure hardship. Anyone whose ears can withstand the sound made by all these young high-pitched voices deserves to have the people on stage clap for him, not the other way around.

After he has mastered these lessons, Dad sees his kid on the stage and realizes that true talent comes from the genes. There couldn't be any doubt because every student had an equal opportunity to shine, but his kid's performance is by far the best of the show.

Finally, he learns that some fathers don't appreciate great talent and appear no more interested in his kid than he was in their kids when they were on the stage.

Fido Is Father's Best Friend

From the day they pick up the family dog at the pet store, Dad never has to wonder why a canine is called man's best friend.

Consider one thing the dog does that no one else will ever do: It will watch whatever Dad wants to see on television. No one else could ever live up to this high standard.

There's more to the argument. Consider what the family dog does not do: It won't object to going out because it doesn't have a thing to wear, doesn't come over to drink all his beer and doesn't expect him to watch home videos of its offspring on their vacation.

In fact, some fathers find canines are easier to look after than young children. This might seem rather callous but it should be pointed out that dogs drool only on hot days, rarely keep everyone awake at night and don't have to be burped after every meal.

But the best thing about a dog is that it can go to an obedience school. Even if it is a slow learner, it is likely to learn enough to please Dad. It doesn't have to know every possible trick. Dad is quite satisfied if it can learn to greet him with his slippers when he arrives home as well as to come when called, sit when ordered and be quiet when asked; by mastering these commands, it is a step ahead of his kids.

Of course, Dad pays a price for having someone around the house who listens to him. He has to take care of the dog after it has been in the family for a week. The promise the kids made at the pet shop to feed, walk and bath the dog doesn't last long.

Naturally, Dad is prepared to do the work, but he does wonder from time to time whether an obedience school would be a good place to send his kids.

Dad Loses By A Whisker

There is a myth that most fathers do not like cats. This is not true. They just dislike having to live with one. A father living in one city has nothing against the cats in another, or anywhere else in the country. Nothing at all. In fact, the farther away a cat is, the more Dad likes it.

Other members of the family do not understand Dad's attitude. They think he should like a family pet that has to be let into the house in the middle of the night, scratches furniture it did not buy and trips him in the hallway when it is racing to get its food. Furthermore, the rest of the family thinks Dad should like an animal that won't come when called, won't chase a ball and can't be trained to fetch his slippers or the newspaper.

In fact, the family cat is so self-absorbed that it can't understand why the dog does any of these things. The cat realizes there is no point doing tricks if it's going to be fed anyway.

As far as Dad can see, cats have only one advantage over dogs: they clean themselves. If they were able to teach children how to do this, they would be worth the fuss everyone else makes over them.

But cats can't be bothered showing anyone anything. They are so independent that if they had hands that enabled them to get the cat food by themselves, they wouldn't bother being around humans at all.

The most annoying characteristic about the family cat, however, is its response to Dad's attitude to it. Completely disregarding his feelings, it jumps onto his lap when he is wearing his best pants, purrs and insists that it be petted. The more Dad tries to ignore it, the more it comes to him.

This is not done as a sign of affection. Far from it. It is meant to be infuriating. And it is. This taunting and teasing puts Dad in a difficult position. If he shoos the thing away, he risks having everyone in the family accuse him of cruelty. If he doesn't, he'll be covered in cat hair. Either way, the cat knows that it has outwitted him.

The Cottage Industry

Cottage dads deserve sympathy. Most of them inherited their cottages from their parents and they can't escape the class into which they were born.

These fathers spend their weekdays working at their offices or plants and their evenings working around their homes. Then they go to their cottages on the weekends where they work harder than anyone on a chain gang from the moment they arrive until the moment they leave.

The work, in fact, begins long before they arrive at their so-called havens. It begins as soon as they leave their urban homes and get into their cars. Just look at the highways on a Friday evening. They're jammed with thousands of other dads driving to the cottage. On most trips, cottage dads declare every other driver to be an idiot who must be practising for the Indianapolis 500. Their patience is further strained because all they hear from the back seat is,

"Are we there yet?" And, naturally, they are required to stop at every gas station for a washroom break.

Once they are at their cottages, they are expected to cut the grass, repair the shutters, replace old shingles, remove broken windows, paint the walls, cut firewood for the barbecue and catch the raccoon under the cottage without hurting her.

While doing all these chores, they are also expected to look after at least a dozen kids. Most cottages come with kids — those who are part of the family and those Dad has never met before. They apparently were invited to come for the weekend but no one bothered to tell him.

But, no, it's not all work. Cottage dads are entitled to take off Labor Day, providing they have the cottage ready for winter.

The lucky fathers who stay in the city during the weekends at least have the opportunity on hot days of going to a pool to cool off. Cottage dads might be only a stone's throw from a lake, but they're far too busy to put a toe in the water.

It would be easy to suggest that legislatures pass laws abolishing cottages so that these cottage dads could live normal lives. Tempting as this notion is, it would never be accepted by their children, whose idea of a perfect life is to go to a cottage and loaf around.

These children might not be so enthusiastic if they could look ahead 30 years and realize who will be doing the work then.

Breaking Camp

The best thing Dad can say of a camping trip is that it enables him to be nominated for an Academy Award for pretending in front of a camcorder to be enjoying himself. He acts as if there is nothing wrong with leaving the comforts of the city for the harsh outdoor life and getting only a few hours of sleep at night.

Lighting the fire to cook the meals would be a chore even if the previous campers had left any twigs around. It usually turns out that the logs purchased on the way to the camping ground are damp and have been turned into homes for bugs. The only way to get good dry wood is to go all the way back home to get the logs left over from the fire on Christmas Eve. Dad, naturally, volunteers to get them. Who else is going to get up at 6, return to the city and be back by 10 to take the kids swimming?

The day-time tasks, nonsensical though they may be, are easier to accept than the night-time duties. No child under the age of five has ever been known to go camping without having to be escorted to an outhouse just after his dad has fallen asleep.

But that's not all. Sometime during at least one night Dad is always awakened by everyone declaring that they heard a bear and wanting to know what he is going to do about it. He says the noise is not from a bear but from a farm dog. The possibility doesn't occur to anyone except Dad that if the sound did come from a bear, he would do more harm by disturbing it than by leaving it alone. Nevertheless, to soothe everyone's nerves, he gets up, finds the dog a mile away and returns to find everyone asleep.

The one real advantage of camping is that after the inevitable downpour, the family makes a unanimous decision to spend the rest of the holiday in a motel where the food is cooked, the sheets are dry and there are no bears. Dad no longer has to act as if he is enjoying himself because he is.

A Recipe For Disaster

Considering that Dad has never been accused of impersonating a chef, he has a problem when he is left alone with the kids for the weekend. Nobody eats well.

The easy solution would be to order Chinese food for breakfast, lunch and dinner. This solution, however, is too easy. Dad, always trying to do his duty rather than take the easy way out, decides to please all members of his family by offering to cook whatever they want. To start with, he asks everyone what they would like for breakfast and finds that everyone wants a different kind of cereal. Naturally, the only place that has all of the requested items is a grocery store, not a regular home. Having been promised whatever they want, the kids now regard Dad's reluctance to rush out to the grocery store as a breach of trust.

After the cereal disaster comes another disaster: the eggs. This starts harmlessly enough with one of Dad's jokes. He says he can cook any kind of egg. The joke is that he means either brown eggs or white eggs. The kids fail to see any humor in the comment and expect him to cook any kind of egg that they want.

No two children want their eggs the same way. Boiled, scrambled, poached, fried. By this time, Dad has lost his sense of humor. He wants to crack eggs, not jokes.

How, he wonders, is he supposed to cook every different style of egg without using every single saucepan and frying pan in the house? In frustration, he changes his mind and announces that he is making only boiled eggs. That should end the debate. Of course, everyone has a different concept of the ideal boiled egg. He is told that the white and the yolk should be soft; the white should be hard and the yolk soft; the white and the yolk should both be hard.

And this is just breakfast. The thought of Chinese food for both lunch and dinner starts to have a certain appeal. Even chefs have to know when to call for help.

Dad Always Flips

During the summer months, there's one ritual that can be seen every Saturday evening in every neighbourhood — fathers barbecuing the supper. Of course women are capable of operating a barbecue, but you won't find many of them out with hamburger flippers. Dad won't give up this job; this is his job.

Dad's attraction to barbecues is intriguing because even today many men don't know a great deal about cooking. Some profess to have an allergic reaction to handling food, except when they eat. But most fathers spring to life the moment the barbecue comes out.

It must be primordial. The first cavemen understood that their role in life was to do the dirty jobs and so looking after the fire pit was part of their job description. Only those fathers with the ability to get a fire going quickly ate enough to survive and pass on their genes. Things haven't changed that much. If Dad doesn't get the barbecue going quickly, he will be in big trouble.

Of course, with the proliferation of gas barbecues, the problems fathers once had with fire pits and even charcoal barbecues have been relegated to history. Now, all Dad has to do is open the gas tap and push the starter button. But he still has to put up with the heat, the fumes, the grease and the kids changing their minds three times about whether they want hamburgers or hot dogs and whether they want their food well-done, very-well done, medium, medium-medium, medium-rare or rare. In comparison, getting the fire started by rubbing a couple of sticks together was a lot easier.

As the days become shorter and he thinks about putting the barbecue back in the garage for the winter, Dad knows that whatever else may happen in the year ahead he can count on flipping the hamburgers again next summer. It's always a dirty job but someone has got to do it and everyone knows who that is.

Mouse Tales

By now, Dad has been able to get the PC at home up and running but he'll never be mistaken for a computer whiz. He still doesn't think in the language of computers. For him, a ram is an animal, and so is a mouse. A virus is something that might give him a cold. Memory is something he might be losing.

But the kids learn how to operate a computer even earlier than Dad expected. On a Saturday morning, for example, he might let his youngsters sit on his knee while he slowly and carefully clicks on the mouse as he does his weekly banking. He thinks he is helping them become familiar with a computer so that they will know how to operate one by the time they are in high school. Little does he know how intently they watch what he does. If he leaves the computer to pour himself a coffee, they can swiftly click on the mouse and move all the money in his savings account into the little savings accounts they have for money they get at Christmas. With his assets now wiped out, Dad has no alternative but to call the bank manager on Monday morning in an attempt to rectify the problem. The manager may be quite reasonable, particularly if he or she is old enough to remember the good old days when young children merely played with their parents' bank books. The manager will, however, suggest that from now on Dad should know where his children are whenever the computer is on.

By the time the kids are 10, their skills are at an advanced stage. They know how to break into the bank's main computer system and are on the way to breaking into other key computer systems, such as the one the American military uses to keep track of its weapons. If World War III starts, it will not be because of the Russians, who don't have any good computers, but because Dad thought the kids were just joking when they sat at the computer and said they were about to fire a missile.

Dad tries to keep up with his kids' knowledge of the computer, but it is a hopeless quest. They may spend five hours a day playing on it. He is lucky if he can spare five minutes a week, which is not even enough time to warm up the computer. But if he asks his kids to help him learn more, he will be told the only way for him to learn is by doing the task himself. These words will sound familiar to him.

Of course, if he ever feels that he has mastered his computer, the next generation of PCs will be in the stores and he'll be expected to bring a new one home. The only thing trickier than keeping up with the next generation of computers is keeping up with the next generation itself.

The Cutting Edge

No matter how long the grass is, Dad has noticed that the kids always have something else to do whenever he asks them to cut it. The longer the grass, the more things they have to do. This concept has been tested by so many fathers and found to be true that it qualifies not just as a theory but a scientific law. In fact, there has never been an exception.

Dad will be told, for example, that his teenage children have to do their homework. Homework is important but whenever the kids go inside to do it they act as if they are doing a project on the length of time friends spend on the phone, the ability of teenagers to tolerate music played at a high decibel level or the effect of television shows upon youth. Dad, of course, is most reluctant to interfere with their education by asking them to set their project aside and come back out.

To be fair, Dad realizes that the kids don't always use the line about homework. During July or August, the excuses are more creative. This is when he hears all the medical problems, such as having an allergic reaction to grass that is exacerbated by cutting it. Although he doesn't want them to do anything that would aggravate an allergy, he does observe that grass does not appear to produce the same allergic reaction when it is underneath them during a ballgame at a park. He also doesn't understand why the kids haven't asked to see an allergist.

Gradually, Dad starts wondering if he should accept at face value what he is told. He concludes that the long-term solution to getting help with the grass lies not with the kids but with the high-tech world. If hardware stores could start selling robotic lawnmowers, all he would have to do is buy one and then get the kids to put in the appropriate disc early in the spring.

Until the day when these robotic lawnmowers are available, Dad fears that he will have to continue mowing the lawn. He knows he can't come up with any excuses Mom would accept.

The Winning Goal

Every spring, Dad's thoughts turn to his first love: road hockey. Drive around any city, town or village and you'll see fathers racing up the side of the road trying to catch up with a tennis ball that just bounced off an old hockey stick. "Run! Run! Shoot!" Nothing is going to stop them. They won't slow down even if they are out of breath.

It doesn't matter whether they have sons or daughters because every father is entitled to play road hockey. During these few moments, the burdens of raising a family are forgotten. This is the height of Western civilization.

The older Dad gets, the more he realizes that road hockey is even better than ice hockey. No one keeps any statistics to prove who scores the most, and with no video camera above a goal crease, he may claim as many goals as he likes. In fact, no one remembers the score two minutes after the game ends.

But it isn't just the game that appeals to Dad. It's the dream — the fabulous dream he had when he was 10. Then, when he played road hockey he was Gordie Howe, Maurice Richard or Frank Mahovlich. "There's Mahovlich, racing toward the net. He shoots. He scores!" Those were the best days in Dad's hockey career. He peaked at 10.

It didn't matter that hockey for these men was a way of getting money to buy cars, groceries and their children's clothes; they were heroes who were sacrificing body and soul for the noble cause of defeating rival teams that dared to think they were good enough to be in the same league as his team.

For a while, Dad is a kid again. By the next day, the game is a memory, but his sore muscles linger for a long time. His dream now is about a time when that didn't happen.

Dad Is A Swinger

For Dad, the occasional trip he makes to a golf course should be an enjoyable summer experience, an opportunity to have a break from looking after his children and to spend quality time with his friends — assuming that trying to hit a little ball into a slightly larger hole over and over again counts as quality time. Alas, even this pleasure is spoiled by all the jokes he has to suffer.

In fact, society's attitude toward his pastime is so negative that Mom is described as a "golf widow." Good grief! At the time he feels most alive, she is supposed to think he's no longer in this world.

The cynics are wrong when they say that golf doesn't provide much exercise. Dad has to stretch at least 18 times when he picks up his ball from the cups, and he flexes his right arm several times in the clubhouse after he finishes the 18th hole.

And he knows that the cynics are wrong when they say golf is not a contact sport. He has made countless contacts on the fairways. Where else is he supposed to go to meet new customers?

The people who mock him and his summer game don't realize that golf does more to keep him healthy than any other sport. He may talk to every doctor in town just by showing up at the golf course on Wednesday afternoons.

Dad, as usual, modestly declines to justify his time on a golf course. He'd rather let his caddie carry the argument. Golf gives Dad the chance to slow down, relax and feel the sunshine, something he should do more often.

But perhaps Dad is wise not to bother trying to justify one of his few pleasures in life. He knows he's not going to persuade anyone to think differently. His best strategy is to treat the jibes as being par for the course.

The Big Leagues

The fathers of children between four and 16 have at least one stressful activity on the weekend: they coach minor sports teams. The amount of energy the average father spends on coaching is equal to that devoted by Tony LaRussa during a tough year.

The sport doesn't matter. It may be soccer, baseball, hockey or football. Once Dad has a child, he instantly becomes an athletic adviser.

Fathers watch particularly closely for signs that their children have athletic potential, such as an ability to put a baseball glove on a hand, a helmet on a head or a pair of skates on the proper feet. With signs such as these, Dad would not be doing his duty if he did not prepare them to be Olympic champions and professional athletes, even if the kids next door are faster and stronger.

And so Dad has no choice but to volunteer to be a coach of his children's teams. On Saturdays, his day begins at 6 a.m., when he gets up to review the lineup and strategy that he thought out at 2 a.m. before he went to sleep. He has to make sure he is being fair to the kids of other parents who have entrusted him with this great responsibility, but he still wants to make sure he doesn't short-change his own kids by not playing them enough.

By 7 a.m., Dad is mentally exhausted but running on adrenaline. He can't stop. He is sure that Sports Illustrated in 20 years' time will mention his name as being one of about 100 people who had some influence on his family's athletic accomplishments. You don't get that kind of recognition without making some sacrifices.

By 8, he's going over the strategy with the team, demonstrating on a chalkboard how victory is assured.

By 9, the game is under way. The strategy is brilliant. All the team has to do is follow it. They may be having a little difficulty implementing the strategy because the other team seems to have its own strategy, but this is no reason to doubt the wisdom of his plan.

By 10:30, the game is supposed to be over. But it isn't over for Dad. He's going to play it again and again in his mind. Win, lose or draw, he will analyze the game without the benefit of video tape replays. This goes on until 11:30 at night and resumes when he wakes up the next day, Sunday. He continues to analyze the game until 11 a.m. when he goes to church. Even then, his interest in his team doesn't cease. He takes a few moments to seek divine intervention to bolster the team's scoring potential in the next game.

It is no exaggeration to say that the feeling of responsibility felt by every dad who coaches is as great as that felt by LaRussa before a big game. At least LaRussa gets paid for the stress.

For his efforts, Dad isn't paid anything. He's lucky at the end of the season if the kids even remember to thank him. They're already thinking about the next sport they want to play.

The Party Line

The telephone was invented to help all humans communicate, but in homes with teenage kids, Dad knows it has failed to meet its potential. It makes everyone in the family so angry that they refuse to speak to one another. According to the kids, the person responsible for this frustrating situation is Dad. He has the notion that because he helps to pay the phone bill he has some right to use the telephone some of the time.

The kids become particularly upset when Dad uses this argument about paying the bill. They see it as unfair. They regard any attempt to restrict their right to communicate with the outside world as a violation of the Geneva convention on the treatment of prisoners. But, no matter what arguments they advance, he will not budge from his fundamental position.

Dad is doubly blamed because he encourages them to have friends and then he pretends to be surprised when they and their friends want to talk on the phone hour after hour. It is enough to make Dad wonder if he erred in not encouraging his kids to be loners.

Dad is prepared to accept one small compromise: He is willing to put in writing the circumstances when he insists that he has the right to use the phone. The kids may have it at any other time. The rule is that a person on the phone must give it up if another member of the family has an emergency call to make. With this clear rule, the family should cease having trouble over the phone.

Later, however, it becomes apparent that this solution is flawed because the word "emergency" is subject to different interpretations. To his daughter, it includes seeking help when she is trying to decide what to wear. To his son, it includes seeking information about getting to a beach. To Dad, it has a narrower definition. It means calling the police or booking a tee-off time at the golf course.

Because of these various interpretations, it becomes apparent that the only answer to the telephone problem is to give the kids a separate phone line to their bedrooms. This solution does cost more money but it is worth the cost because it improves the communications between Dad and the kids.

Bouncing Through Life

From Dad's viewpoint, there are a few advantages to having a trampoline in the backyard as opposed to having one in someone else's yard. The reason, of course, for *not* wanting one of these monstrous contraptions that takes up the entire backyard is obvious: a trampoline is a monstrous contraption that takes up the entire backyard.

But the advantages are important. First, Dad can make sure it is properly constructed. He feels morally responsible for his kids' safety and so there is no question who has to build it. If his kids are going to use a trampoline to blast off the Earth with the thrust of one of NASA's rockets, the least he can do is make sure it is more or less properly constructed. Nevertheless, he will have less than half an hour after the trampoline arrives to assemble it the way the instructions recommend. After that, if he hasn't managed to get it up, his kids will — without reading the instructions.

Even if he has other pressing business, the best deal he can make is to promise to put up the trampoline in 20 minutes if the kids will find all the tools he needs for the job. This may be the only time in his entire life that they will quickly do what they are asked to do.

The second advantage to having the trampoline in his yard is that Dad gets to give the safety lecture. He discusses the rule stressed in the manual: one person on the trampoline at a time. Asked if they understand the rule, they say nothing but have little smirks on their faces. Dad realizes he asked the wrong question. Of course they understand the rule. They do understand English and they can count. They just don't want to follow the rule.

The final reason why Dad is prepared to have a trampoline in the yard is different. Late at night when the kids are in bed, he can go out and have a little fun himself.

Money Problems

As Dad knows, when he gives an allowance to his kids he gets nothing but problems in return. The only exception occurs when the children are very young. Until the kids are five, he can happily hand over nickels and dimes with the assurance that they will be left on a coffee table where he may collect them and give them again next week. After the age of five, however, the kids become sophisticated. When they notice that their piggy bank isn't growing, they become quite agitated and start gathering signatures for a petition complaining about the financial system once again being unfair to the little guy.

From then on, the kids check how much Dad gives them each week. It is never enough. There is always someone on the block who receives more. This attitude is ungrateful, but Dad should be leery of condemning it too strongly. It is apparently a pre-requisite for high-paying salaries, such as those given to professional athletes. No one gets those jobs by saying thank you for a paycheque.

Dad just shrugs his shoulders and offers what he can, along with a requirement that at least a minimal amount of work be done each week, regardless of the moaning that this requirement produces. "The more you work for your money, the more you'll appreciate it," he says — which is a pleasant thought but one that has no empirical evidence to support it.

This requirement makes discussions about allowances more complicated than ever. In fact, they aren't discussions; they are labor negotiations. Was the work done at all? What penalties are appropriate if it isn't? Does homework count as a good excuse for not doing chores that were assigned two weeks ago? Does having a cold mean that sick pay must be given? Is forgetfulness a legitimate excuse for not doing a job because it could be an early warning sign of a serious loss of memory?

Dad decides that he should offer an incentive plan and treat the kids as partners in a family firm. This means that he bases their allowance on the amount of work completed. Even this arrangement, however, is less than perfect. It assures that all chores are done in record time, but it doesn't take into account the quality of the work. The dishes may all be washed and put away, but they are not necessarily clean after leaving the sink or dry when entering the cupboard — or even put in the right cupboard. At this point, Dad gives up.

The problem ultimately goes away when the kids get part-time jobs and don't need an allowance. At that time, they will have more free money than Dad has seen since he was a teenager doing part-time jobs.

Dad's Part-Time Job

In most families, fathers eventually reach the age when they have to learn about the working world. This comes when their teenage children seek their first part-time jobs.

This process takes a lot of Dad's time but only some of the teens' time. It starts with the preparation of a resume. As Dad knows, it has to be done so well that it would impress a headhunter looking for a chief executive officer of a multi-national corporation. It doesn't matter that the job involves flipping hamburgers. What matters to Dad is that his kids learn to do resumes so well that they will never fail to be employed, and, consequently, will never again have to rely on him for money.

Dad has to work hard to bring the resumes up to this high level. Creative thinking is required. For the section on education, for example, Dad may have to suggest that his kids say they have done a lot of independent study in order to cover the fact that they have been suspended from almost every school in the city.

Then Dad has to coach the kids on what to say during the interview: Always say the job is required to get the money to go to university. This impresses most employers because they realize that a good employee has to make creative use of facts when talking about the company's product or service. What better way for an applicant to demonstrate this skill than by saying the money is needed for educational purposes? Employers are smart people. They know the kind of educational purpose the money will be spent on: teen magazines, CDs and movie tickets.

Once the kids have their jobs, Dad really goes into overtime. He has to drive them to and from the hamburger joint. Naturally, the kids have the worst possible shifts — the ones that the owner, being an adult, doesn't want. The owner isn't nuts. He doesn't want to be at the store at midnight. He's home sleeping.

Of course, Dad gets in the car at 10 minutes to midnight in order to pick up his teenagers because the alternative is worse: The youth squad of the police department finds them, thinks they're abandoned kids, brings them home and delivers a stinging lecture about leaving kids out on their own in the middle of the night.

If Dad adds up the cost of the driving and pays himself minimum wage for all the time he spends helping, he would find that the kids' jobs are a net financial loss to the family. Now that he knows so much about the working world, the thought occurs to him that he would have done better if he had been the one flipping the hamburgers.

Danger Ahead

After years of driving everyone around town, fathers are always delighted when their kids go to the licence bureau to get a learner's permit. Dad now has a wonderful opportunity to demonstrate his driving skills, but this optimistic mood doesn't last long. No matter how great he is as a driver, he does not know how to teach anyone how to drive. It's like baseball: Just because a ballplayer can hit a ball doesn't mean he can teach another person how to hit anything.

The problem is compounded by the driving instructors. They mean well. They know the rules — and this can be very frustrating.

Just when Dad is demonstrating how to signal a lane change, his teenage son or daughter feels morally compelled to point out that Mr. Smith, the driving instructor, would not approve of changing lanes in such a dangerous manner. Mr. Smith said good drivers put on the turn signal 3.5 seconds before switching lanes. Dad signaled only 2.7 seconds before changing lanes, as may be proved by the stop watch brought along for this very purpose. He is also accused of letting the car go six inches past the white line marking the spot where he should have stopped at an intersection and of having only one hand on the steering wheel while he switched on the radio.

There are no good answers Dad can give to these accusations. If he says he has been driving this way for 20 years, he will be told that it is hard to believe he hasn't been in numerous accidents.

Dad quickly acknowledges that he has to change his driving habits so that Mr. Smith would be impressed. Only when he makes this pledge does he feel that his teenager will not call the police to report a dangerous driver roaming around the city's streets. After Dad fine-tunes his knowledge of the rules of the road, he resumes his attempt to supplement the formal lessons given by that know-it-all, Mr. Smith.

The truth is that there is no easy way to teach someone to drive a car, just as there is no easy way to teach someone to ride a bicycle. Dad's way of avoiding a catastrophe is to point out every upcoming traffic light a mile in advance. He also feels obligated to say when every one is red, just in case his teenager turns out to be color-blind. There is no point finding out about this medical condition by going through an intersection at the wrong time.

These sessions are stressful. Very stressful. They are so stressful that Dad quickly changes his opinion of Mr. Smith. Dad is now delighted to pay him any amount of money he would like to get this job done.

Dad Loses His Car

When his teenage kids get their driver's licences, Dad thinks he has become a free man. No longer does he have to chauffeur the family around town to all the places that are not on a bus route as well as many that are. But this feeling doesn't last long. He just slips from one form of bondage into another.

Dad had assumed that because the car was registered in his name, he had some right to drive it. This was a false assumption. He now finds himself in the unenviable position of not having a vehicle to transport himself. The teenagers have countless places to go to that are more important than any of his destinations: They have to go to the beach, the movies, the dance.

Whereas previously the kids had to check with him to arrange a ride, he now has to check with them to see if he is allowed to have the car. If he can't

have it, they let him know if and when they can pick him up.

Let's not exaggerate. The kids do not prevent him from having the car to go to work. They are not crazy. Teenagers don't want to stop any parent from going to work and bringing home money that they can borrow whenever they so desire.

It would also be unfair to suggest that teenagers do not understand the problem caused by their ability to drive. They are quite aware of it and they have a solution: another car.

Dad agrees and says that he had been coming to the same conclusion. It quickly becomes apparent, however, that they had a different view of the new car. He had been thinking that the kids would buy it; they had been thinking that he would. He had been thinking of a cheap, third-hand car purchased with the money from their part-time jobs; they had been thinking of a Corvette purchased with whatever money he wants to provide.

This slight difference in the appropriate car and the appropriate method of payment gradually enlarges until Dad says that he cannot buy a Corvette unless he uses the money he had put into his retirement fund. Failing to grasp Dad's sarcastic tone, the kids accept the offer and thank him for his generosity.

When told what the word sarcastic means, they feel deflated, but they realize that he has a point. If he spends all of his retirement fund, they would have to look after him in his old age. He also realizes that a third-hand car is not a solution. It would forever be breaking down and they would expect his car to be kept available as a backup.

Eventually, everyone comes to a sensible conclusion: Instead of either a new car that he buys or a third-hand car that they buy, Dad agrees to help them buy a second-hand car by providing them with a loan. Had this compromise not been accepted, he feared that the alternative was that he would have to buy a bus pass.

Body Language

There isn't a father who hasn't seen tattoos and earrings all over his teenagers. Some dads see them in real life; others see them in nightmares.

They know that many earrings have no more contact with an ear than an earwig and end up in a nose, eyebrow, tongue or navel. In fact, a father who previously might have wondered why his son wanted an earring might now be thankful if it goes in an ear.

If Dad asks why earrings aren't for ears, he is likely to be told that if he has to raise this question, he won't understand the answer, which is probably true. If the conversation goes any further, he will be told that it has something to do with individuality. If nothing else, all members of the family can agree on that.

Furthermore, Dad will be told that there is nothing wrong with putting earrings everywhere because an ear, nose and throat specialist on TV said the ear is connected to everything else. It is questionable, however, whether the good doctor expected a general comment to be interpreted in this manner.

The natural reaction of fathers when confronted with the imminent appearance of body art in the family is to resort to sarcasm. They are inclined to suggest that teenagers who are really interested in art should visit an art gallery. Sarcasm, however, can backfire. In this case, it is likely to be the inspiration for a tattoo of the Mona Lisa.

There is only one argument Dad can give that has any persuasive power in discouraging his kids from having tattoos and earrings all over the place: "Think about it. You can always get one in the future." By the time the future comes, the fad will have faded and Dad will have other issues to deal with that are more than skin deep.

Cool Clothes

Every year with the arrival of winter, Dad can perform a test to check the maturity level of his kids. All he has to do is see what they wear outside on a cold day. If they put on sweaters, jackets, scarves, mitts, hats and boots, they are still young and mature; if they put on nothing but T-shirts, jeans and running shoes, they are growing up and not very mature at all. This is a difficult stage in Dad's life: How easy life used to be when the kids could be stuffed inside snowsuits and wrapped in scarves.

Watching his teenage kids go out with little, if any, protection from the cold makes Dad doubt the concept of human progress and whether humans have any more intelligence than monkeys, who at least are smart enough to be born with fur coats. He also wonders about his ability to communicate what he thought was a simple phrase: "It's cold outside."

There is nothing wrong, however, with his speech or their ears. They hear everything Dad says on this subject. They just have other priorities. For teenage girls, putting on a coat would hide the fashion statement being made that day with a blouse or sweater; for teenage boys, it would simply be uncool. No further argument is apparently needed. Dad's comments about cold weather are dismissed as the tiresome observations of the older generation.

Oh, the doctors have their explanations for the way the kids behave. They talk about the thyroid gland at the base of the neck increasing the Basal Metabolic Rate and they say this gland works better with young people than with old folk, which is why older people feel the cold more.

Well, sure, this explains why teenagers don't feel the cold in quite the same way that older people do, but it doesn't explain why they pretend not to feel cold at all when it's 10 below zero.

Dad would be happy if the doctors would learn how to cure a deficiency of common sense. Then he wouldn't have to worry about whether his kids pass or fail his maturity test each winter.

Splitting Hairs

Hard as it is to accept, the bald truth is that all kids seem to enjoy teasing their dads about grey hair and receding hairlines. Children who would never make a politically incorrect joke see nothing wrong with cranking out one-liners about Dad's hair.

He is told that the only difference between him and a bald-headed eagle is that the eagle can fly without getting in a plane. These jokes — or rather so-called jokes — never stop.

The irony is that the very kids who mock him are the ones who caused him to lose his hair in the first place. But the kids' jokes are particularly irksome to many dads today because hair meant so much to them when they were younger. They still remember the days when their hair went down to their shoulders and parted their generation from their parents. Long hair was a symbol of youth.

Dad's first response to this onslaught of jokes is to start combing the strands of hair that he does have over the parts of his head that don't have any. It ends with him going to his doctor to talk about transplants and drugs.

Although every father has the right to do what he wants with the outside of his head (others apparently have the right to decide what goes on inside), it is time that fathers ceased worrying about this problem and came up with a means of dealing with it permanently. There is a perfect strategy and it has three components: Deny, deny, deny. Denial has the advantage of being the most inexpensive way of dealing with the loss of hair.

Dad has to argue indefatigably that this is not an issue on which there can be any shades of grey and he is not going to split any hairs. His hair is as thick and dark as ever.

If he needs a witness to help him defend his position, all he has to do is ask his barber whether he sees any sign of a receding hairline or a grey hair. It's amazing how a barber can give the right answer when he thinks it will increase his tip. The barber's response may not reverse Dad's receding hairline, but knowing that he has at least one supporter makes the kids' jokes easier to accept.

Rolling Along

The Rolling Stones are preventing Dad from enjoying one of the privileges of middle age: the right to rant about the music and culture of his kids.

Whenever he goes on a tirade about some modern freaky singer such as Marilyn Manson, the Stones spoil his speech by going on another tour, reminding everyone that they were as slovenly as any group today. Every time Mick Jagger gets up to sing, he casts doubt on Dad's observation that the culture of the '60s was the height of western civilization as well as civilizations that were eastern, northern and southern.

The passing of time hasn't mellowed these boys. Granted, the word "boys" is somewhat inappropriate because they have aged a bit. By now they must at least be in their 30s. But there they are. Cigarettes dangle from their lips, defiance flashes in their eyes and so many lines are etched on their faces that if you read between them you'll see a bad novel. They still get up on stage, hit their guitars and drums, and croak out their rough songs. They'll bang out Satisfaction, even though their former fans are now more interested in getting satisfaction by rolling their retirement portfolios into successful emerging-market funds than in any way the Rolling Stones originally suggested.

There never was much depth to the Stones, a point Dad might not have realized when they were in their prime. Of course, at that time the only credential anyone needed to be a philosopher was to have long hair and to look scruffy.

The Stones represent the part of the '60s that, most of the time, Dad is happy to forget. They are the part that was tough, wild, churlish and rebellious. Apart from this annual nostalgic tug that occurs when the Stones go on tour, Dad would be just as happy if they could find a way to gracefully — well, gracefully by the Stones' standards — wander off into musical history. Dad could then talk about the glory and purity of the '60s. Then, he would be free to rant about Marilyn Manson.

No Room to Move

Dad usually obeys the law, but he knows that his house contravenes the municipal zoning bylaw because his teenage kids' rooms are not fit for human habitation.

Indeed, Dad hardly ever goes in them. If he tries to go into one, his first task is to find the doorknob, which is not an easy chore because the door is covered with more posters than the foyer of a movie theatre. If he is lucky, he finds the doorknob in about 10 seconds.

Even after he finds the knob, he cannot get the door to open. Something is blocking it. When he points out that he cannot get in, he is told that he should push harder. After Dad expresses a few appropriate words, the occupant of the room realizes that he may have a point. There may be a knapsack on the floor behind the door, even though no one seems to know how it got there.

When Dad finally gets inside, he wishes he hadn't. He can't believe his eyes: the room is in even worse shape than it was the last time he looked in. There is no sign of a floor. There are candies, candy wrappers, three empty bags of potato chips, a box of crackers, a half-empty soft drink bottle, dirty clothes, clean clothes, hangers, shoes, plates, glasses, mugs, jewelry, a photo album, knickknacks, books, pens, pencils, a CD player, discs, computer printouts, the family's extra computer, a telephone book, a telephone with the receiver off the hook, a curtain that came down, blankets, sheets, a wet towel, a dry towel, a desk drawer and, finally, there is a garbage pail — with no garbage in it.

Dad dare not take another step. Using diplomatic language, he notes that the room does not seem to be perfectly tidy. He receives an undiplomatic answer. He is informed that he is stifling individuality by expecting others to live the way he does, that he is trespassing on private property and that he should produce a search warrant if he wants to make another appearance.

Dad suggests that the next time he tries to enter the room, he will come with a bylaw inspector to get the room condemned as a health hazard. It is an empty threat. He knows the inspectors are only interested in working on problems that have a chance of being resolved.

Worry When The Kids Listen

There is a common belief among fathers that teenagers will not listen to them. This is not true. They listen whenever they want to.

They listen, for example, when Dad speaks about the principle of a fair day's pay for a fair day's work. Naturally, not wanting to disappoint him, they firmly request professional rates for cutting grass, shovelling snow and taking out the garbage. If they really want him to feel like a great employer, they seek payment for answering the telephone because one of the calls might be for him. To do anything less would be to break all sorts of labor laws.

They also listen when Dad talks about the importance of friends. Friends, he always says, will be lifeboats that will help when times are tough. Of course, to keep these lifeboats in good shape, they must not be cast adrift. They need care and attention. This requires regular visits in — guess what? — Dad's car. No errand he has before him could possibly be more worthy of the car than his teenagers' need to be with their friends on Friday and Saturday nights. Oh, no, they don't want to hang out just for fun and to have a good time; they want to see their "lifeboats."

And they listen when Dad suggests they should be back home by midnight and not on the streets where danger lurks. Only because of Dad's concern for their safety do they feel forced to hold parties in the living room that start at midnight and go through the night. Of course, Dad realizes that it is far better to have the CD player blaring in his living room where there is no noise bylaw, far better to have a few pop bottles around where there are no notices about littering, far better to have his house upside-down than someone else's.

After the party is over, the kids remember what Dad always says: They should get lots of sleep, thereby enabling their growing bodies to become stronger. This advice, they presume, applies even if there is a mess to clean up.

Even if Dad has to do the job first thing in the morning because the party-goers are all asleep, the cleanup provides him with a chance to remember the parties he once went to. He knows the common belief teenagers have about their fathers never being young isn't quite true.

The Kids Have The Power

By the time Dad realizes that his kids are running his life, he has to face another harsh truth: they have the right to vote and are running the country. This is a traumatic revelation.

He only just finished showing them how to make an "X" along with all the other letters of the alphabet when, suddenly, for no reason other than the fact they are 18, they have the right to make an "X" on a ballot. Surprisingly, their ballots count as much as those marked by an adult. Dad now thinks that the kids *should* be going out at night, carousing around and having a good time before they have to worry about societal problems such as whether pensions should be increased for people who will retire in the not-too-distant future — that's the kind of question he's happy to answer.

Instead of spending their time the way Dad now suggests, the kids during an election campaign listen keenly to all the candidates and read the pamphlets of all the parties. This provides proof that they are not ready to vote. It shows that they can't make up their minds.

Understandably, he is concerned that the kids might be inclined to vote for someone who panders to younger people as opposed to someone who panders to older people, which is entirely different. It's a matter of maturity.

The existence of politicians who think all votes are equal is enough to make him think the vote should either be taken away from 18-year-olds or that a law should require them to vote the way their fathers recommend. Either option would end the trauma.

Dad's College Education

Dad doesn't realize how little he knows until his kids are old enough to go to college or university. In fact, considering his lack of knowledge, he is amazed that he has been able to survive as well as he has, let alone raise a family.

The most important thing he learns is that he doesn't know anything about higher education. It is, he is told during the later years of high school, boring and pointless. For a while, universities and colleges aren't as exciting as the thought of getting a job at minimum wage that provides enough money to buy the necessities of life — a few CDs and stylish clothes. However, after countless discussions on the value of higher education, the kids finally agree to submit applications to a university or college. In fact, the discussions weren't all that important. They decided going to a post-secondary institution wasn't such a bad idea when Dad said he would help pay their tuition but would not pay for them to go to Los Angeles while they waited for Hollywood to recognize them as stars.

Even after they accepted Dad's offer, Dad is deemed to know little about institutions of higher learning. It is true that information about courses, programs and fees does change, but a fundamental fact remains the same: The application is supposed to be sent in advance of the deadline. The kids, however, hadn't bothered to put the date on the calendar. They don't worry about this, though. They know they'll get in. They tell Dad to phone the registrar's office and say he has just written a cheque for the alumni association.

With everything sorted out and the day approaching when the big move to the campus occurs, Dad suddenly becomes slightly more knowledgeable. He does know how to transport books, pens, paper and clothes to a student residence: in his car. It is certainly a better method than using an inter-city bus.

Once at the institution of higher learning, the kids quickly forget their doubts and angst, but they don't forget that Dad is the banker of both first and last resort. Like the federal government, he may go into debt but he is always expected to have money for worthy as well as unworthy projects. These years provide Dad with the opportunity to consider whether it is always better to give than to receive.

As he suspected, the kids' courses turn out to be acceptable, but he does sigh a little when told that the real incentive to come back the following year is the great social life on campus. He hopes that the parties aren't as great as the ones he remembers, but he's glad that they have some compelling reason to continue their studies.

The Perfect Wedding

The father of a bride has traditionally been accorded little respect at weddings, but this doesn't stop him from attending, even if he has other important things to do. He should really be "the best man" because he's supposed to provide the cash to make the whole thing happen, but his largess produces not respect but pity, particularly if he has an entire family of daughters.

The problem is that Dad has no decision-making power. He's told who his daughter is marrying. He's told he can't even invite his drinking buddies despite the guest list swelling to 200. He's even told when he has to walk down the aisle.

This lack of respect doesn't take into account the subtle but vital role Dad performs the days immediately preceding, and during, his daughter's wedding. As the wedding day approaches, he is the only person in the entire house who is calm enough to re-member the details. Everyone else is exhausted. What a shame it would be if weariness prompted the bride to forget to go to the church on the wedding day.

He tried to warn everyone that they would be tired if they continued staying up until 2 a.m. every night during the week before the wedding. Every-one else lost sight of the importance of being wide awake at the wedding so they could make it a joyous event for the guests.

Instead of conserving their energy, all other mem-bers of the family and the wedding party run around mailing invitations, sewing dresses, baking cakes, ordering limousines, arranging flowers, calling the photographer, getting a marriage licence and going to the jewelry store to pick up the wedding rings.

The mother of the bride stays up later than any-one. She is almost frantic. She acts as if a wedding is supposed to be a once-in-a-lifetime event. Con-stantly mentioning that there are hundreds of things still to do makes everyone feel more stressed than they already were. While all this fuss is going on, Dad is peacefully in bed, resting up for the big day.

Dad's calm approach is most noticeable on the wedding day as he swiftly puts on his tuxedo. No fuss. No stitches. No last-minute panic attack caused by the realization that he ordered it before losing weight, or that he failed to lose weight after ex-pecting to. And his hair is fine the first time he combs it, even if by now he doesn't have much.

With everyone around him announcing another crisis or predicting the next one, he carries on, telling people in the wedding party how wonderful they look despite their lack of sleep.

Dad's foresight was wise. He is well-rested. The bride is so exhausted that she would never be able to navigate the entire length of the church aisle without the support of his arm. He is, in fact, so well rested that he could carry her if necessary.

Mom is no help. While Dad is saving the wedding, an usher leads her to a pew to sit down because she is too tired to participate.

Of course, the wedding turns out perfectly. Friends and family rush over to say what a wonderful day it was, but Dad turns down all offers of congratulations and says, humbly, that all the credit should go to everyone else.

Every Day Should Be
Father's Day

With Dad spending so much time with his children, our society requires a new way of honoring his contribution to his family. There is, however, no point suggesting that he be paid for his efforts. Even if some government could find the money — which would be difficult considering the enormous value of his contribution — he would spend it on his kids, if he even got to see the cheque.

There is also little point in suggesting that the kids pledge to do something extra special for him on Father's Day. This is a well-intentioned but ill-conceived proposal. Having a day set aside for Dad each year is really tokenism and may be harmful to his health. He can't cope with the sudden change from being a serf to being the lord of the manor on the third Sunday of June. This is the cold-turkey approach to honoring Dad. It will always be a shock to his system. Furthermore, on the day after Father's Day, Dad becomes a serf again, which is especially hard because he has just seen how he should be treated.

Of course, Father's Day wasn't meant to be this way. In fact, Sonora Smart Dodd wanted nothing but good to come out of her campaign to have a day set aside each year for fathers. While listening to a Mother's Day sermon in a church in Spokane in 1909, she wondered why there was no Father's Day. The question arose in her mind because she knew her father, William Jackson Smart, had done more than a little work around the house. He was a widower who had raised six children after his wife died in childbirth. Sonora succeeded in getting the support of the Spokane Ministerial Association and the YMCA to have a special day for fathers.

Today, most fathers probably feel they are working even harder than William Jackson Smart. So thinking men — and that is not an oxymoron despite what some misguided people say — see no alternative but to celebrate Father's Day every day of the year. Not surprisingly, they expect the United Nations to pass the appropriate declaration giving moral support to this radical idea in every country. The preamble will provide the philosophical justification: "Fathers, having helped raise the next generation by sacrificing body and soul and many hours at the pub, golf course or ballpark, deserve more respect than they have received."

With this declaration, fathers will no longer feel that they are serfs and they will know that liberty, equality and fraternity can indeed be found in this world. Best of all, they may find that they can use this declaration to have a little time to themselves. Who could ask for more? Certainly not Dad.

Knowing Dad, he is likely to feel slightly embarrassed by his new status. But why should he? He has earned this honor.

Come to think of it, there isn't any need to wait for a formal declaration that Father's Day be celebrated every day. The citizens can lead the politicians on this issue. The principle behind the declaration may be implemented even if the UN spends its time debating other important subjects. Like good manners, this new concept of Father's Day may be applied anywhere at any time, particularly at home when Dad is there.

All that is needed is an appreciative word. Ties, golf balls or any of the other gifts associated with Father's Day are not required. At first when the kids tell him each day how much they appreciate him, Dad might suspect that they are just trying to get him to do something for them. But, for once, his suspicion will be wrong. He'll have to put his understandable reaction aside and gradually get used to the idea that every day is going to be Father's Day.